The Smart Little Crab

Written by Kerrie Shanahan

Illustrated by Susy Boyer

Flying Start
to Literacy®

Contents

Chapter 1
Home by the sea

On the rocky shore next to the sea there was a rock pool. In the rock pool lived many plants and animals.

It was a good place to live because
the rock pool was clean and healthy.
All the animals lived happily with
each other in their rock pool.
That was, until the sea star got bored.

Chapter 2
Sea star's bright idea

"I'm bored with our rock pool,"
said the sea star. "It's always
the same. The tide comes in.
The tide goes out. Day after day.
Our rock pool is boring and I'm
bored too!"

The animals looked around and
started nodding.

"I have an idea," said the sea star.
"Let's fix up our rock pool. Let's
make it look sparkling and new."

"Yes!" said all the animals.
"Let's fix up this boring old place."

"But, but wait," said the little crab.
"Our rock pool is not boring. This
is how a rock pool is meant to be.

We have everything we need.
We can hide amongst the seaweed.
We have fresh seawater coming in.
The seawater brings lots of little
animals to eat. Don't change it!"

But no one was listening. All the
animals had gone to find new things
to put in their rock pool.

Chapter 3
Trash or treasure?

When the animals came back, they had new things for their rock pool.

"Look, I have a shiny new tin can," said the sea star as he put the can on top of some seaweed. "Now we have somewhere to sit."

"But the tin can is squashing the seaweed," said the little crab.
"We need the seaweed for food and for a place to hide. Where will we hide and what will we eat when the seaweed is dead?"

But no one was listening.

The sea snail family arrived with
an empty plastic bag.

"Wow," said all the animals.
"We can make a roof out of that."

So the animals put the plastic bag
over the rock pool.

The little crab just watched and
shook his head.

"That plastic bag is dangerous,"
he said. "Our baby animals could
choke on it."

But no one was listening.

Then the octopus pulled a big box
into the rock pool.

"Look," she said. "This will be great
fun to play in."

The little crab was shocked.
"That will stop the fresh seawater
coming into our rock pool," he said.

"The fresh water brings us lots of little animals to eat," said the little crab. "What will we eat instead?"

But no one was listening.

Chapter 4
An exciting new rock pool

The animals gathered more and more bits and pieces to add to their rock pool.

They dragged and lifted and pushed and pulled all the new things.

They worked hard to make sure
that their rock pool was not
boring anymore.

"Look at our rock pool now," said the
sea star. "We have so many new and
interesting gadgets to play with."

"Yes," said the other animals.
"It looks wonderful."

But the little crab did not think
their new home was great.

He looked around the rock pool.
He wondered how this could have
happened to his beautiful,
healthy home.

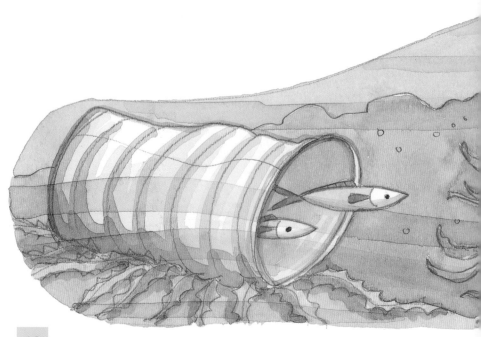

"Our rock pool is very different from how it used to be," said the little crab. "I'm worried that it will not keep us all healthy anymore."

But no one was listening.

Chapter 5
Trouble in the rock pool

For some time, the other animals were happy in their new home, but then the rock pool started to change.

The water got dirty and the seaweed
stopped growing because no fresh
water came into the rock pool.
Finally the other animals could see
what was happening.

"Our rock pool is dying," they all
cried. "What will we do? How
can we save our home?"

Chapter 6

The little crab speaks up

"LISTEN TO ME!" said the little crab in his biggest, loudest voice. "I know what to do. We must clean up our rock pool. We have to get rid of the things that do not belong here."

At last the animals listened
to the little crab.

They began to clean up their
rock pool. It was hard work but
the animals were determined
to have a beautiful, healthy rock
pool again.

They dragged and lifted and
pushed and pulled until all
the rubbish was gone.

It took time but eventually the
rock pool was clean again.

And from then on, whenever the
animals had a new idea, they always
checked with the little crab first.